## This Little Explore The

## book belongs to:

______________________________

# For
# Curious Learners

Published by Grant Publishing

Sales and Enquires: grantpublishingltd@gmail.com

**FOLLOW US ON SOCIAL MEDIA**

60
FACTS
ABOUT
COLOMBIA

# 60 Facts About Colombia

Hello, little explorers! Do you love learning about faraway places and cool facts? Well, have you heard about a land full of captivating stories, charming cities, and delicious food? It's called Colombia, and it's one of the most fascinating countries in the world!

If you want to know more about Colombia and its wonders, there's a super fun book you must read. It's packed with interesting facts that are as delicious as treats and stunning photos that will leave you in awe. So, sit back and get ready to take a journey to Colombia through the pages of this book!

# For Parents

We know that reading a book about a new country can be an exciting adventure for your child. It's important to remember that kids need breaks, and may not want to read the book all in one sitting. Encourage them to take breaks as needed, and ask them questions about what they've learned so far. Discussing the facts with your child can help them remember and retain the information better. You can also use the book as a springboard for further exploration and learning about Colombia. Perhaps you can plan a family outing to try some Colombian food or visit a local museum with exhibits on Colombian culture. Above all, we hope that this book sparks your child's curiosity and inspires them to learn more about the world around them.

# MAP

Manizales
Bolivar Peak
16,427 ft
Cúcuta
Medellín
Maracaibo
Valencia
Maracay
CURAÇAO
Bogotá
COLOMBIA
Pasto
Cali
Quito
ECUADOR
Cuenca
Chimborazo
20,702 ft
Guaviare
VENEZUELA
Orinoco
Mt. Roraima
9432 ft
San Felipe
Boa Vista
Iquitos
Napo
Arica
Piura

# The Facts

1. Colombia is a transcontinental country spanning South America and North America.

DID YOU KNOW?

2. Colombia is officially the Republic of Colombia.

SOUTH AMERICA IS A DIVERSE AND VIBRANT CONTINENT, KNOWN FOR ITS STUNNING NATURAL LANDSCAPES, RICH CULTURAL HERITAGE, AND INCREDIBLE BIODIVERSITY. FROM THE MAJESTIC ANDES MOUNTAINS TO THE LUSH AMAZON RAINFOREST AND THE VIBRANT RHYTHMS OF SAMBA IN BRAZIL, SOUTH AMERICA OFFERS A CAPTIVATING BLEND OF BREATHTAKING BEAUTY AND CAPTIVATING TRADITIONS.

## 3. Colombia is bordered by Venezuela, Brazil, Ecuador, Peru and Panama.

HOW MANY CAPTITAL CITIES CAN YOU THINK OF?

## 4. Bogota is the capital city of Colombia.

*Pictured Bogota, Colombia*

## DID YOU KNOW?

*Guatapé, located in Colombia, is a charming town famous for its stunningly painted buildings adorned with intricate designs and colorful murals.*

**5. Colombia is 1,141,748 square kilometres.**

**6. Colombia is the fourth largest country in South America.**

*Pictured Guatape Town, Colombia*

## 7. Colombia has a population of roughly 50 million people.

## 8. Colombia is the second most populous country in South America after Brazil.

## 9. Bogotá has over 7 million inhabitants.

Visitors in Bogota can expect to immerse themselves in a bustling metropolis filled with historical landmarks, vibrant street art, and a thriving culinary scene.

## 10. Bogota is also the largest city in Colombia.

## 11. Spanish is the official language of Colombia.

**COMMON PHRASES IN COLOMBIA**

1. *Hola (oh-lah) - Hello*
2. *Gracias (gra-see-as) - Thank you*
3. *Por favor (por fah-vor) - Please*

## 12. There are also 65 Amerindian languages spoken in the country.

## 13. The national anthem of Colombia is 'Himno Nacional de la Republica de Colombia'

The Colombian national anthem, titled "Oh, Gloria Inmarcesible" (O Unfading Glory), was written by Rafael Núñez and composed by Oreste Sindici. It was officially adopted as the national anthem in 1920.

## 14. People from Colombia are called Colombian.

15. The motto of Colombia is 'Libertad y Orden'.

¡Oh gloria inmarcesible! ¡Oh júbilo inmortal!

16. Colombia gained independence from Spain on 20th July 1810.

DID YOU KNOW?

Colombia gained its independence from Spanish colonial rule on July 20, 1810, marking the beginning of a long and challenging journey towards establishing a sovereign nation.

## 17. The currency in Colombia is the Colombian Peso.

**Did You Know?**

*The Colombian peso is the official currency of Colombia, represented by the symbol "COP." It is used for all financial transactions within the country and comes in various denominations, including coins and banknotes.*

## 18. In Colombia, people drive on the right side of the road.

## 19. Colombia's economy is the third-largest in South America.

*The Colombian flag features three horizontal stripes of yellow, blue, and red. The yellow stripe represents the country's wealth and resources, the blue represents the two oceans that border Colombia, and the red symbolizes the courage and valor of its people.*

## 20. The national flag of Colombia features three horizontal stripes of color, or tricolor. The top half is yellow, and the bottom half is split into two stripes, one blue and one red.

## 21. People have lived in Colombia since at least 12,000 BCE.

*Pictured Cartagena de Indias, Colombia*

## 22. Groups like the Muisca, Quimbaya and the Tairona have lived in Colombia since the first millenium.

### DID YOU KNOW?

Colombian history is a tapestry of indigenous cultures, Spanish colonization, struggles for independence, and the challenges of modernization, shaping a nation with a rich heritage and diverse cultural influences.

23. The name 'Colombia' is derived from the last name of the Italian navigator Christopher Columbus.

24. The Spanish arrived in 1499 and colonized the region and called it New Granada.

## 25. Colombia is one of the most ethnically diverse countries in the world.

## 26. The majority of Colombians are Roman Catholic.

Colombia is home to numerous breathtaking churches, showcasing a blend of architectural styles and religious significance, with notable examples like the Salt Cathedral of Zipaquirá and the Las Lajas Sanctuary, attracting visitors from around the world.

## 27. Football is the most popular sport in Colombia.

*The Colombian national football team, known as "Los Cafeteros," is celebrated for its passionate style of play and has achieved success on the international stage, captivating fans with their skill, determination, and love for the game.*

## 28. The traditional national sport of Colombia is called Tejo, a team sport that involves launching objects at a target which contain gunpowder and explode on impact.

**29. The Black and White Carnival is one of the most popular festivals in Colombia dating back to 1607.**

**30. The Carnaval de Barranquilla is a popular festival in Colombia.**

## DID YOU KNOW?

Carnaval de Barranquilla: Considered one of the largest carnivals in the world, Barranquilla's carnival is a colorful celebration of music, dance, and folklore, featuring parades, costumes, and traditional music genres like cumbia and vallenato.

31. Colombia is known for its lively salsa music and dancing. Salsa festivals and competitions are held throughout the country, where dancers showcase their skills and the infectious rhythm of salsa fills the streets.

32. Many regions in Colombia celebrate the Semana Santa (Holy Week) leading up to Easter with religious processions, reenactments of biblical events, and traditional ceremonies.

**33. Colombians have a strong coffee culture, and the National Coffee Festival is celebrated annually in Manizales.**

**34. Colombia is the third largest exporter of coffee in the world.**

Colombia is renowned for its exceptional coffee, known for its rich flavours, smoothness, and aromatic qualities, making it a favourite among coffee enthusiasts around the world.

## 35. Colombia is one of the world's seventeen megadiverse countries.

*A megadiverse country is a term used to describe a nation that is exceptionally rich in biodiversity.*

## 36. Colombia's climate is classed as tropical and isothermal.

*Pictured Mountains of Colombia*

## 37. The longest river in Colombia is The Magdalena River.

## 38. The Andes mountain range runs through Colombia.

**DID YOU KNOW?**

Colombia is the only South American country with coastlines and islands along both the Atlantic Ocean and Pacific ocean.

## 39. The highest mountain in Colombia is Pico Cristobal Colon which is 19,020ft high.

**Did You Know?**

*Colombia is home to numerous volcanoes, with more than 15 active volcanoes spread across its territory. One notable volcano is Nevado del Ruiz, located in the central part of the country.*

## 40. There are over 30 volcanoes in Colombia.

**41. Colombia has between 10 and 20% of total global plant species.**

**42. Colombia's national flower is an orchid called "Cattleya trianae".**

## 43. Colombia has the largest amount of endemic species in the world.

**DID YOU KNOW?**

Endemic species are animals that exist only in that country.

## 44. Some endemic animals found in Colombia include the pink amazon river dolphin and brown woolly monkeys.

45. Colombia has the world's largest number of bird species.

46. Colombia is the second most diverse country in the world for freshwater fish.

## 47. Colombia is rich in natural resources. Natural resources found in Colombia include natural gas, gold, coal, copper and petroleum.

## 48. Colombia is known for its magnificent emeralds.

The country's rich mineral deposits and geological conditions contribute to the formation of these stunning gemstones, making Colombian emeralds highly valued for their exceptional color, clarity, and quality.

**49. Colombian cuisine is influenced by indigenous food as well as Spanish and African cooking styles.**

Ajiaco

**50. Many Colombian dishes include maize, rice, seafood and tropical fruits.**

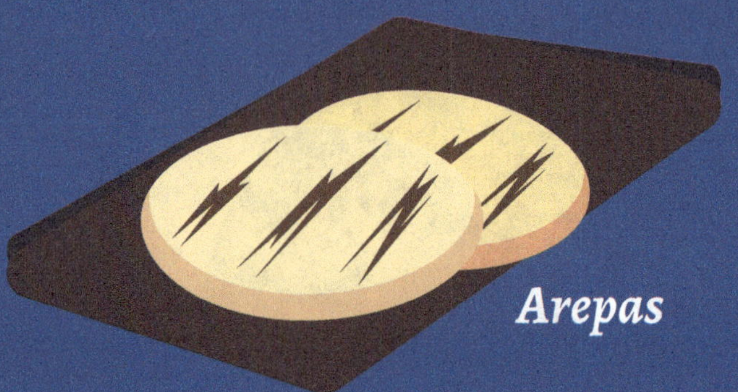

Arepas

The French Alps is home to the Vanoise National Park, the first national park established in France.

## 51. Popular dishes in Colombia include Tamales, Arequipe, Arepa, Chocolate con queso and Changua.

## 52. One of Colombia's national dishes is a traditional Andean dish that originated from Bogotá, called Ajiaco.

### Common Colombian dishes

- Chicharrón - Crispy deep-fried pork belly or pork rinds, a popular snack or ingredient in various dishes.
- Posta Negra - Slow-cooked beef in a sweet and savory sauce made with panela (unrefined cane sugar), coffee, and spices.
- Mondongo - A hearty soup made with tripe (beef stomach), vegetables, and spices, often enjoyed with rice and avocado.
- Ceviche - Fresh fish or seafood marinated in lime or lemon juice, mixed with onions, tomatoes, cilantro, and served cold.

**53. Arroz con Pollo, rice and chicken with a variety of vegetables, is a popular dish in Colombia.**

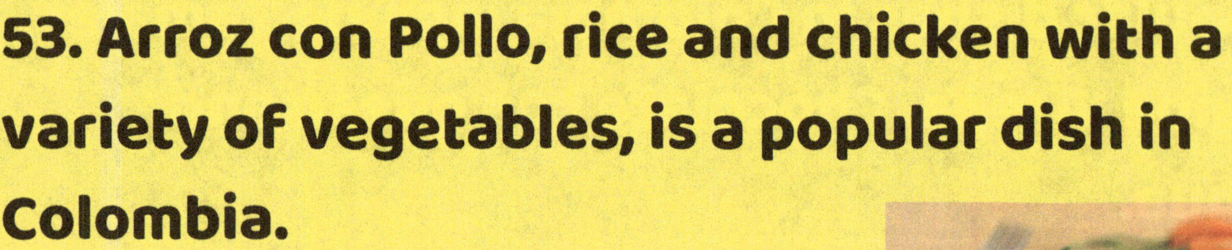

**54. Colombia's tropical climates allows for an abundance of tropical fruit to grow.**

55. Unique fruit also grow in Colombia such as Soursop and Sweet Granadilla.

56. Colombians have a strong sense of community and solidarity. Volunteering and helping others in need, particularly during challenging times, is a common practice and a reflection of their caring and compassionate nature.

57. Respect for elders is an important cultural value in Colombia. It is customary to greet older people with respect and deference, often using formal terms of address such as "señor" or "señora."

58. Bullfighting, although controversial, is a traditional sport in some regions of Colombia.

**59. Colombians are known for their warm and welcoming nature. Hospitality is highly valued, and guests are often treated with great generosity and kindness.**

*Colombia has a rich folklore tradition with mythical creatures and legends. Stories of El Dorado, La Llorona, and the Muisca people are part of the cultural fabric and are often passed down through generations.*

**60. Music and dance are integral parts of Colombian culture. Traditional dances like Cumbia, Vallenato, and Salsa are popular, and festivals featuring vibrant music and colorful costumes are held throughout the country.**

# Places To Go

# Places To Go

Attention, little explorers! Get ready for an exciting expedition to the captivating land of Colombia! It's time to grab your adventure gear, pack your curious minds, and join us as we uncover the hidden gems of this extraordinary country. From the vibrant streets of Cartagena to the lush landscapes of the Amazon rainforest, and from the stunning beaches of Tayrona National Park to the mystical ancient ruins of San Agustin, our book will take you on a magical journey through Colombia. Immerse yourself in the rich culture, taste mouthwatering local cuisine, and encounter fascinating wildlife. So, fellow adventurers, get ready to embark on an unforgettable escapade as we unlock the wonders of Colombia together. ¡Vamos!

Cartagena: This vibrant coastal city is a UNESCO World Heritage site, known for its stunning colonial architecture, colourful buildings, and historical fortresses.

Bogotá: Colombia's bustling capital city offers a mix of history, art, and vibrant urban life. Visit the historic neighbourhood of La Candelaria, home to colonial-era buildings, street art, and cultural landmarks like the Gold Museum.

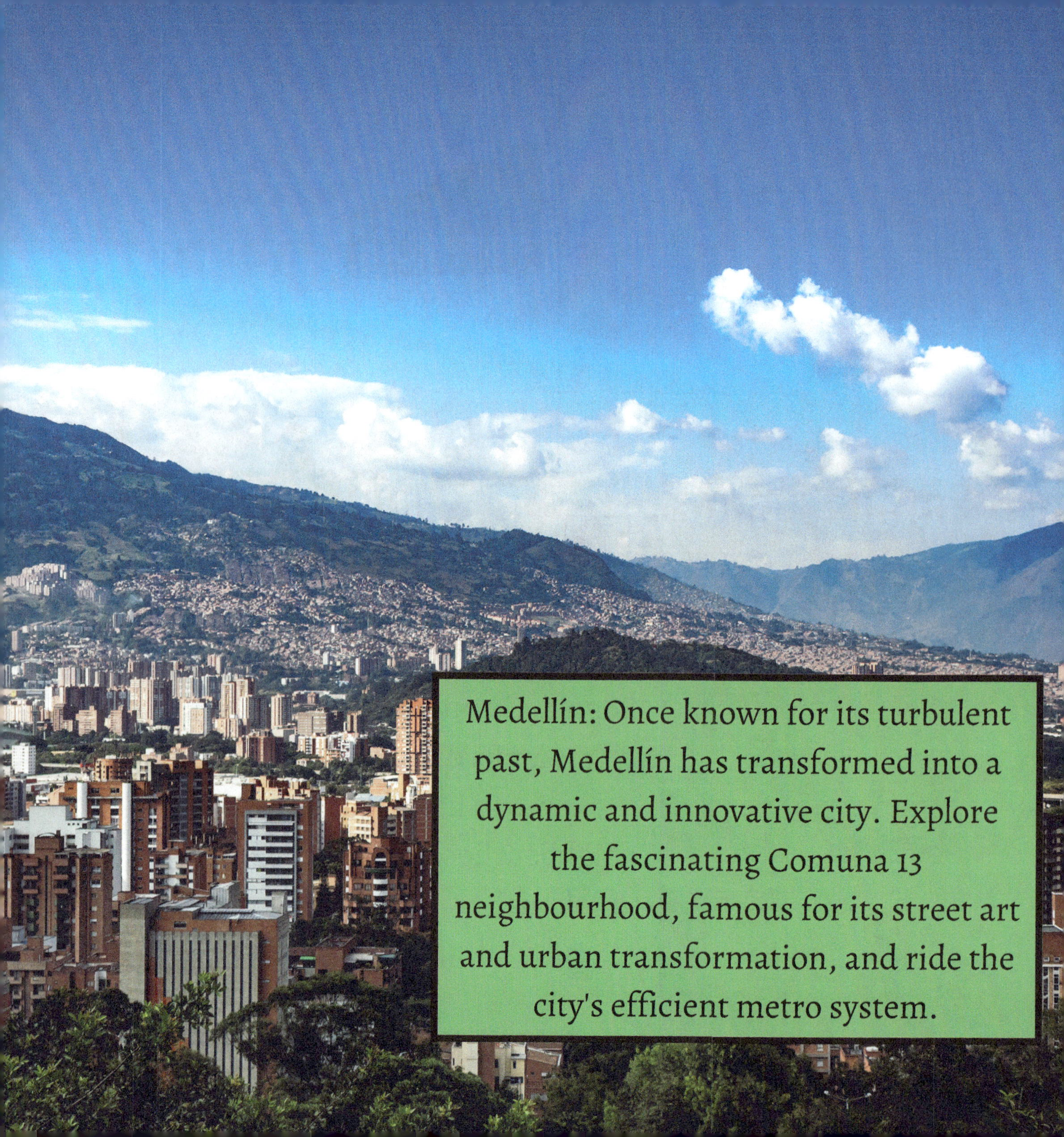

Medellín: Once known for its turbulent past, Medellín has transformed into a dynamic and innovative city. Explore the fascinating Comuna 13 neighbourhood, famous for its street art and urban transformation, and ride the city's efficient metro system.

Tayrona National Park: Located on the Caribbean coast, Tayrona National Park offers a breathtaking natural beauty with pristine beaches, lush jungles, and ancient archaeological sites.

Coffee Cultural Landscape: Explore Colombia's coffee region, known for its picturesque landscapes, coffee plantations, and charming towns. Visit the vibrant town of Salento and hike through the stunning Cocora Valley.

San Agustín Archaeological Park:
Discover the mysterious stone statues
and ancient tombs in the San Agustín
Archaeological Park, a UNESCO World
Heritage site.

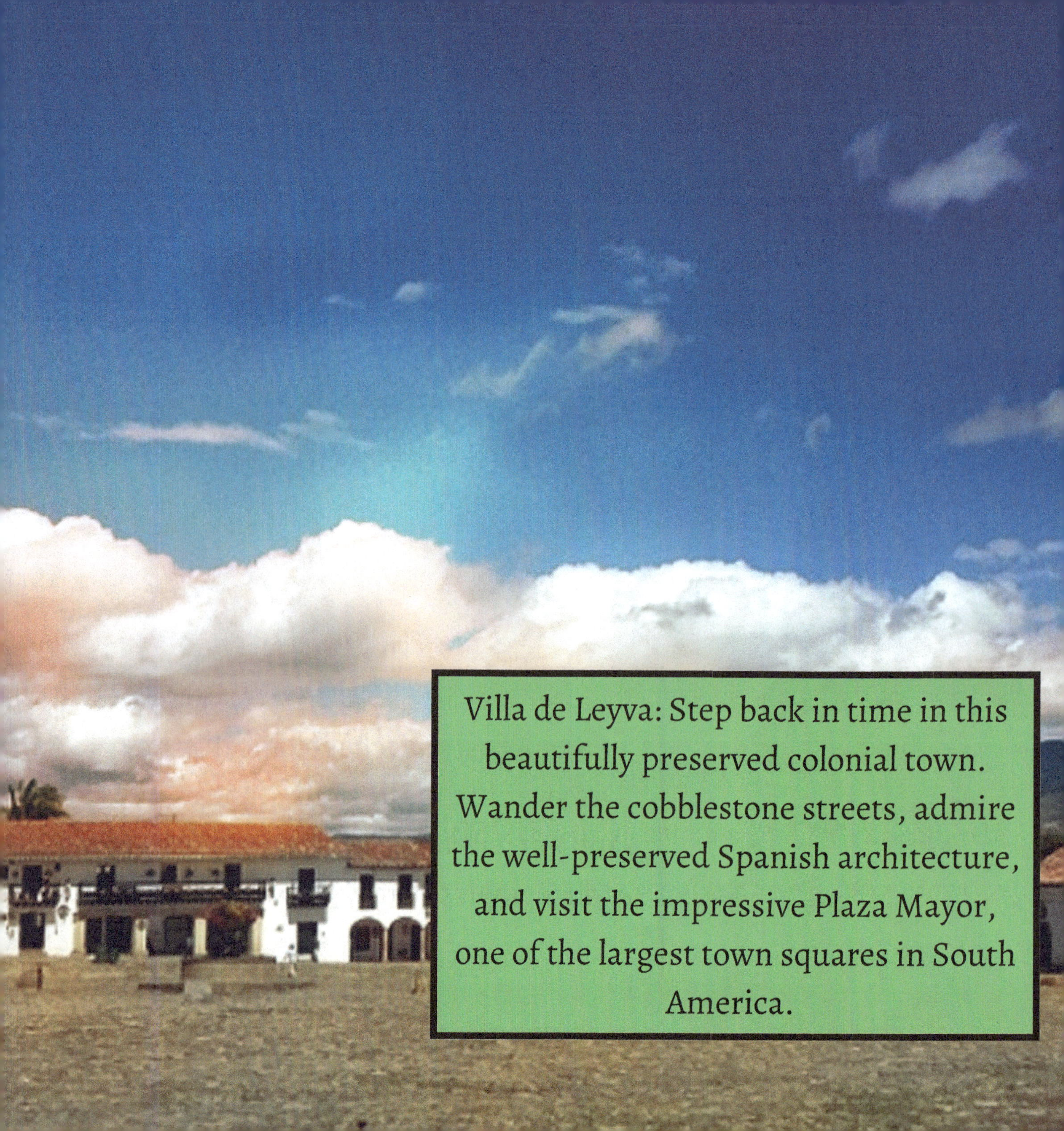
Villa de Leyva: Step back in time in this
beautifully preserved colonial town.
Wander the cobblestone streets, admire
the well-preserved Spanish architecture,
and visit the impressive Plaza Mayor,
one of the largest town squares in South
America.

Guatapé: Known for its colourful streets and stunning lake views, Guatapé is a picturesque town nestled in the mountains.

Ciudad Perdida (Lost City): Embark on a thrilling trek through the dense jungles of the Sierra Nevada mountains to reach Ciudad Perdida, an ancient archaeological site dating back over a thousand years.

Amazon Rainforest: Immerse yourself in the incredible biodiversity of the Amazon Rainforest in Colombia's southern region.

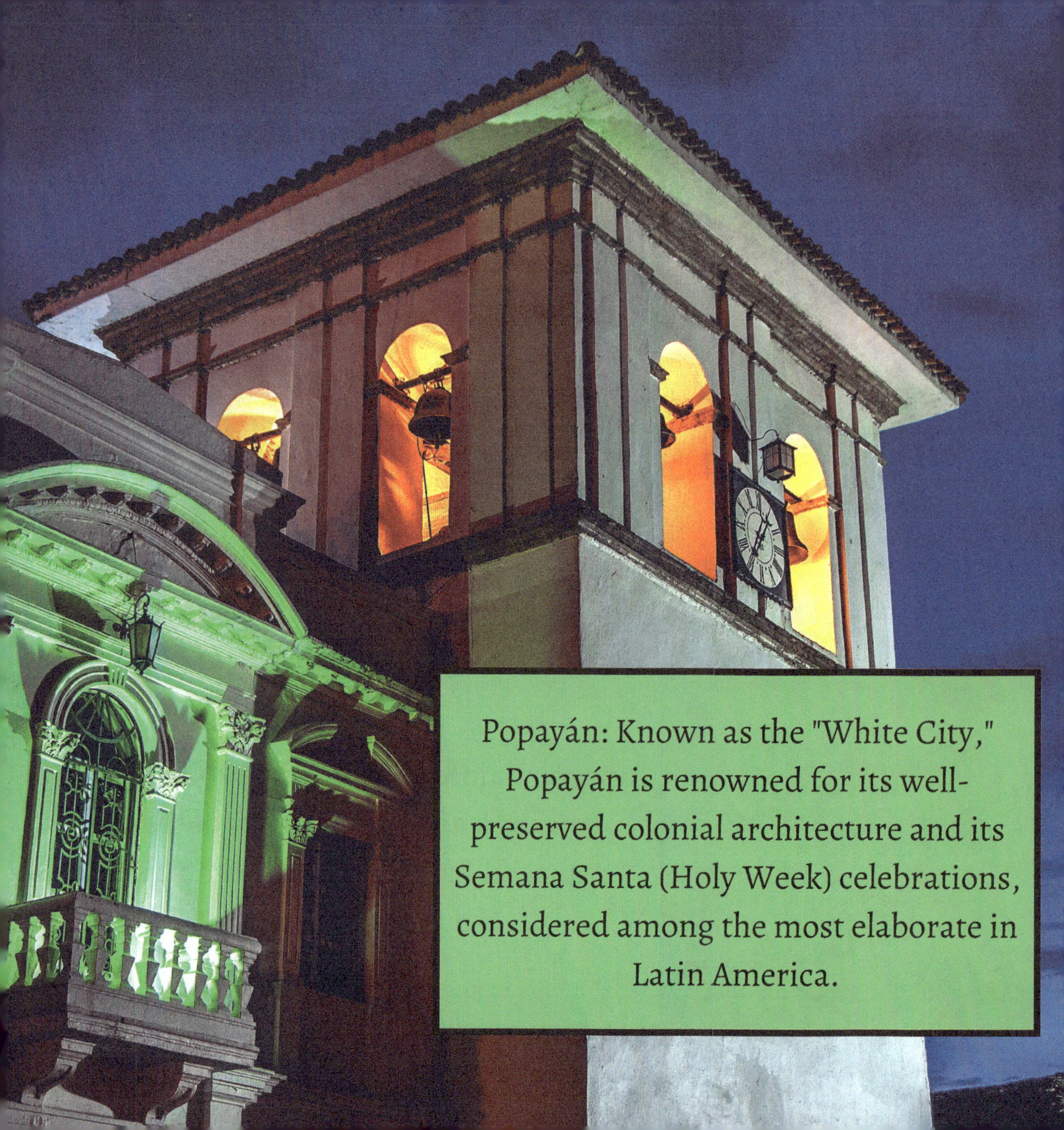

Popayán: Known as the "White City," Popayán is renowned for its well-preserved colonial architecture and its Semana Santa (Holy Week) celebrations, considered among the most elaborate in Latin America.

Guajira Peninsula: Experience the stunning natural beauty of the Guajira Peninsula, located in Colombia's northernmost region.

Providencia Island: Escape to the idyllic Providencia Island, part of Colombia's Caribbean archipelago. Immerse yourself in the laid-back island atmosphere.

San Andrés: Explore the tropical paradise of San Andrés Island, known for its crystal-clear turquoise waters and white sandy beaches. Discover the vibrant marine life while snorkeling or diving, and enjoy water sports such as kayaking and jet skiing.

# Explore

# Explore

Welcome to the "Explore" section! Get ready to put your knowledge to the test with our exciting trivia game about this incredible country. Challenge yourself and your friends with questions about Colombia's history, geography, famous landmarks, and traditional customs. How many can you answer correctly? Don't worry if you don't know them all, because this book is here to help you become an expert on Colombia. So, get ready to have a blast while learning fascinating facts about this beautiful country. Let the adventure begin!

# Test Yourself

Q: What is the capital city of Colombia?
A: Bogotá

Q: Which animal is a national symbol of Colombia?
A: The Andean condor

Q: What is the traditional Colombian dance called?
A: Cumbia

Q: What is the famous coffee-growing region in Colombia called?
A: The Coffee Triangle

Q: What is the name of the ancient indigenous civilization in Colombia?
A: The Tayrona civilization

# Test Yourself

Q: Which famous Colombian painter is known for his vibrant artworks?
A: Fernando Botero

Q: What is the official language of Colombia?
A: Spanish

Q: Which mountain range runs through Colombia?
A: The Andes Mountains

Q: What is the traditional Colombian dish made with mashed plantains called?
A: Patacón

# Activities To Try

# Activities

Bienvenue to the "Activities" section! Here, you'll find a collection of exciting activities that will immerse you in the vibrant culture of Colombia. Each activity is designed to spark your creativity and help you discover the rich traditions and customs of this incredible country. Whether you want to create your own colorful Colombian mask, try your hand at traditional Colombian recipes, or learn some energetic Colombian dance moves, we have something for everyone. So, grab your imagination, put on your dancing shoes, and get ready to embark on a journey of adventure and cultural exploration. Let's dive into the wonders of Colombia together and make lasting memories along the way! ¡Vamos!

# Create Your Own Colombian Flag

Materials needed:

White construction paper or cardstock

Yellow, blue, and red construction paper or coloured pencils

Scissors

Glue or tape

Pencil or marker

Instructions:

1. Take the white construction paper and cut it into a rectangle shape, approximately 8 inches by 12 inches, to resemble the Colombian flag.
2. Using the yellow construction paper, cut out a strip that is about 2 inches wide and long enough to fit across the top part of the flag. Glue or tape it in place.
3. Cut out a blue square from the blue construction paper, approximately 4 inches by 4 inches. Place it in the top left corner of the flag, next to the yellow strip.
4. From the red construction paper, cut out two thin strips, each about 1 inch wide. Glue or tape them diagonally across the blue square to create a cross shape.
5. Use colored pencils or markers to draw a coat of arms in the center of the blue square. You can draw a shield, a condor, and other elements that represent Colombia.
6. Let your flag dry, and then proudly display it or use it for imaginative play..

# Colombian Rhythm Shakers

Materials needed:

Empty plastic water bottles

Rice, beans, or small pebbles

Coloured paper or paint

Glue or tape

Decorative materials (optional): stickers, ribbons, markers

Instructions:

1. Take the empty plastic water bottles and clean them thoroughly.
2. Fill the bottles with rice, beans, or small pebbles. The amount can vary depending on how much sound you want the shakers to make.
3. Seal the bottles tightly with their caps.
4. Decorate the bottles using colored paper, paint, stickers, ribbons, or markers. You can create patterns, draw Colombian symbols, or write your name on them.
5. Let your shakers dry if you used paint or glue.
6. Shake, shake, shake! Enjoy the rhythmic sounds of your homemade Colombian rhythm shakers. You can create your own music or play along with your favorite Colombian songs.

# Colombian Storytime

Materials needed:

Children's books about Colombia or Colombian folktales

Comfortable seating area or blanket

Optional: Colombian snacks or treats

Instructions:

1. Gather a selection of children's books that showcase Colombia's culture, history, or folktales.
2. Create a cozy seating area or lay out a blanket for storytime.
3. Invite your child to choose a book or select one for them to read aloud.
4. Read the story together, pausing to discuss the characters, setting, and any new concepts or words.
5. Encourage your child to ask questions and share their thoughts about the story.
6. Optional: Enhance the storytelling experience by enjoying some Colombian snacks or treats while reading.
7. Continue exploring different books about Colombia, fostering a love for reading and learning about the country's rich heritage.

# Colombian Dance Party

**Materials needed:**
Music player or device
Colombian music playlist
Open space for dancing

**Instructions:**

1. Create a lively atmosphere by playing Colombian music on your music player or device.
2. Clear a space in your living room or backyard to serve as the dance floor.
3. Start the music and encourage your child to move and dance to the rhythm.
4. Demonstrate some simple Colombian dance steps, such as salsa or cumbia, and invite your child to join in.
5. Explore different dance moves together and let your creativity and energy flow.
6. Take turns leading the dance or follow each other's moves.
7. Have fun and enjoy the vibrant and energetic rhythms of Colombian music.

# Learn Basic Spanish Phrases

Materials needed:

Flashcards with Spanish phrases

Pronunciation guide (optional)

Instructions:

1. Introduce children to simple Spanish phrases
2. Show them flashcards with pictures and corresponding French phrases.
3. Practice saying the phrases together, emphasizing correct pronunciation.
4. Encourage them to use these phrases in their everyday interactions.

# Map Exploration

Materials needed:
Map of Colombia
Markers or pencils

Instructions:

1. Provide each child with a map of Colombia.
2. Point out major cities, landmarks, or regions discussed in the book.
3. Help them label and mark these locations on the map.
4. Discuss the distance between their home and Colombia, fostering their understanding of geography.

# Glossary

# Glossary

Amazon - The Amazon refers to the vast rainforest that covers a significant part of Colombia. It is known for its rich biodiversity and is home to numerous plant and animal species.

Bogotá - Bogotá is the capital city of Colombia. It is a vibrant and bustling metropolis with a rich history, diverse culture, and numerous attractions to explore.

Coffee - Coffee is one of Colombia's most famous exports. Colombia is known for producing high-quality coffee beans that are enjoyed worldwide.

Dance - Dance is an important part of Colombian culture. Traditional dances like cumbia and salsa are popular and reflect the country's vibrant and rhythmic music traditions.

Emerald - Colombia is famous for its emerald production. Emeralds are precious gemstones that are mined in Colombia and admired for their vibrant green colour.

Flag - The Colombian flag consists of three horizontal stripes of yellow, blue, and red. It represents the country's values of liberty, equality, and justice.

Gold - Colombia has a rich history of gold mining and craftsmanship. The country has been known for its gold treasures since ancient times.

Indigenous - Indigenous refers to the native peoples of Colombia. They have unique traditions, languages, and cultural practices that contribute to the country's diverse heritage.

# Author's Note

Dear young readers,

I am so excited to have shared with you all about Colombia, a country that is rich in history, art, history, and culture. As an author, I am always inspired by the incredible diversity and beauty of the world around us, and I hope this book has inspired you to explore and learn more about Colombia.

I was inspired to write this book because I believe that learning about different cultures and countries can help us understand and appreciate the world better. It's so important to celebrate and learn from different traditions and ways of life, and I hope this book has helped you do just that.

If you enjoyed reading this book, I would love it if you could leave a review on Amazon. Reviews help other readers discover the book and can make a big difference for independent authors like myself.
Thank you for joining me on this journey, and I hope this book has sparked your curiosity and imagination. Keep exploring and learning about the world around you!

Sincerely,
Grant Publishing